# BLOCKCHAIN

*An In-Depth Understanding of the Blockchain Revolution and the Technology Behind it*

*< Adrian Cooper >*

# Copyright Notice.

©Adrian Cooper

All rights reserved. No part of this publication may be reproduced, distributed or transmitted by any means or in any form, including but not limited to photocopying, recording, or other electronic or mechanical methods, without the prior written permission of the publisher, except in the case of brief quotations embodied in reviews and certain noncommercial uses acceptable to the copyright law.

Trademarked names appear in an editorial style without trademark symbols accompanying every occurrence of trademark names throughout the eBook. These names are used with no intention to infringe on the copyrights of respective owner trademarks. The information in this book is distributed on an "as is" basis, exclusively for educational purposes, without warranty. Neither the author nor the publisher shall have any liability to any person or entity with respect to any loss or damage caused or alleged to be caused directly or indirectly by the information contained in this book.

By reading this document, the reader agrees that Adrian Cooper is under no circumstances responsible for any losses, direct or indirect, which are incurred as a result of the use of information contained within this document, including, but not limited to, — errors, omissions or inaccuracies.

# Table of Contents

Introduction ........................................................................... 1

Part 1: Understanding the Blockchain and the Technology Behind it .................................................................................... 2

Chapter 1: What is a Blockchain? ........................................ 3

Chapter 2: Understanding the blockchain Technology ..... 8

Part 2: Potential uses for the blockchain technology ....... 12

Chapter 3: The Banking Industry ...................................... 13

Chapter 4: Examples of public and private concepts Blockchain . 25

Chapter 5: Financial Services - The Blockchain Innovation .......... 35

Chapter 6: Blockchain Uses - Financial and Non-Financial ......... 46

Chapter 7: Role of blockchain technology in future capital markets ............................................................................................ 47

Chapter 8: Blockchain applications ................................... 55

Chapter 9: Blockchain innovation myths .......................... 67

Conclusion ........................................................................... 76

# Introduction

I want to thank you and congratulate you for purchasing the book,

"Blockchain: Understanding the Blockchain Revolution and the Technology Behind it".

This book contain proven steps and strategies on how to understand fully what a blockchain is, what the revolution is all about and the technology that is behind it all, driving one of the biggest innovations in IT for many years.

You will learn what a blockchain is, and then what the blockchain technology is. I will talk about how blockchain technology is going to change the world we live in irrevocable and forever.

Many of you have probably heard the term, "blockchain", many times over the last few years. That is because it is the technology that underpins the bitcoin, the digital currency that more and more people are turning to. Banks believe that the blockchain could become the future of all financial transactions and governments are being strongly urged to adopt the technology as a permanent and tamper-free way of storing data and transactions.

Now I'm going to take you into the world of blockchain, the technology that drives it and what it means for us in the future.

Thanks again for the purchase of the book, I hope you enjoy it!

## *Part 1: Understanding the Blockchain and the Technology Behind it.*

# Chapter 1: What is a Blockchain?

A block chain is a database that holds a series of records in a list that is ever expanding. Each record is called a block and the blockchain is fully secured from any form of tampering and from revision. Each of the record, or blocks, is timestamped and is also linked to the record before it, hencethe chain.

We all know of blockchains as being the underlying technology of the virtual currency, the bitcoin. The idea of bitcoin was born in 2008 and in 2009 it became a reality and the blockchain is actually a public ledger of every bitcoin transaction. In the case of the bitcoin, each client can connect to the network and can send transactions, and take part inthe heavy competition to make new blocks, a competition known as mining.

**A Brief History**

When it was first thought of, the blockchain really was only for the bitcoin and was derived as the answer to making databases completely secure and with the ability to be distributed widely. From 2014, the term "blockchain 2.0" began to be in the database field and this second-generation blockchain was described by The Economist as having a programmable language that allows users to write more sophiscated smart contracts, thus creating invoices that pay themselves when a shipment arrives or shares certificates which automatically send their owners dividends if profits reach a certain level.

In 2016, a pilot project based on blockchain technology was announced by the central securities depository of the Russian Federations and a number of music industry regulatory bodies have begun to test out models for collection of royalties and copyright management using blockchain technology.

**How Blockchain is Formed**

Each blockchain technology is made up of blocks, each of which holds a valid transaction. Each of the blocks will include a hash of the block before it and this is what links the two together.

These linksform the chain. As well as containing a hash-based history, every blockchain database will also contain a specific algorithm. This is used to score different versions of the histories and this enables one version of higher value to be chosen above the others. Peers that support the blockchain databases do not have access to to the same versions of the history all of the time, instead, they just han onto the version that scores the highest. When a peer gets a newer version with a higher score, it will normally be the one they already have with a new block added to the chain.At this point, they will overwrite the database that they hold and then send the improvement to the other peers. However, there is absolutely no guarantee that one entry will stay in the highest scoring database version forever but, as a blockchain is built to add on the score of a newblock to the total score of the existing blocks, there ia a low probability of an entry being superseded, especially as more blocks go on and because there are certain incentives to working in adding new blocks to extend, rather than working just with old blocks.

**Decentralization**

By the very fact that a blockchain stores data across the network, it cuts out the risks that always go with centrally held data. This is because the network does not have the centralized points that are

# BLOCKCHAIN

vurnerable, and this means hackers cannot exploit them. We all know that the internent has a torn of security problems today; how many of us still rely on the system of usernames and passwords to protect data and identity and these are easily hacked whereas the blockchain uses encryption technology for security.

Encryption technology is based on a system of private and public keys. The public key is a long string of numbers, generated randomly and this is the blockchain address of the user. The transaction that goes across the network is recorded on that key and is and is down as belonging to that specific user.

The private key, on the other hand, is similar to a password and it is what allows the owner access to their digital assets. If you store data on a blockchain, it cannot be corrupted but you will need to take some extra measures – you need to create a paper wallet, and print your private key to safeguard it.

Every single node that is contained in a decentralized system contains a copy of blockchain. There is no official centralized copy anywhere and no one user is given anymore trust than another. All transactions are sent to the network through the use of the software. Mining nodes are then used to validate each of the transactions and then add them to the blockchain that is being created. The entire block is then sent to the other nodes. Each change is serialized through the use of timestamps.

In the beginning, blockchains are used to be permission less and this has led to a certain amount of controversy over whether a permissioned database containing chained data blocks should actually be known as a blockchain. This is an ongoing debate and the crux of it is whether private systems that have verifiers who are tasked by and authoritized by a central authority should actually be a blockchain.

Those in favour of a private chains say that the term "blockchain" should be applied to all data structures that put batches of time stamped data because the blockchains are a distributed version of multi version concurrency (MVVC). MVVC will not allow two transactions concurrently make any modifications to an object within a database and, in the same way, blockchains also stop two transactions from spending a single output within a blockchain.

Opponents say that a permissioned blockchain looks very much like a traditioned database and doesn't support decentralized data verification. These systems are not safe from tampering and are not secure from being revised by the operators. According to the our business review, "a blockchain is a distributed ledger or database that is open to anyone" and computerworld says that most of the hype that surrounds blockchains is nothing more than "snake oil and spin"

**Applications**

The blockchain technology, which I will talk about in more detail later on, can be integrated into several areas, including digital currency, payment systems, crowd sale facilitations, implementation of prediction markets and generic tools for governance. Major blockchain applications include:

**Cryptocurrency:**

- Bitcoin
- Ripple
- Blackcoin

# BLOCKCHAIN

- Nxt
- Dash

**Blockchain platforms**:

- Factom – distributed registry
- Mainsafe-software for decentralized applications
- Gems – decentralized messaging
- Stori- distributed cloud
- Tezos-decentralized voting

**Applications**

According to a research project carried out over 2 years, blockchain technology can be used to store and host, in a secure environment:

- Money
- Titles
- Deeds
- Music
- Art
- Intellectual property
- Scientific discoveries
- Votes

## Chapter 2: Understanding the blockchain Technology

There is absolutely no doubt that the focus, which was once on one crypto currency, is quickly moving towards applications that are based on crypto currency and are built on a blockchain. The technology of the blockchain is almost the same as in the database, but with one exception, the way we interact with them is different.

This technology and space are new, and therefore there are many ways

To understand the block systems and terminology are not yet standardized. In its

The simplest form, the block-chain acts as a joint, replicated, added database

Where access to the record is shared between participants, but verification is performed

All participants. Taking elements common to most chain systems, there are:

A data warehouse, usually containing financial transactions, but can contain any types of data:

Replicating data across multiple systems in real time

Peer-to-peer network topology instead of hierarchical client-server models

# BLOCKCHAIN

Use of cryptography and digital signatures to confirm identity, authenticity and

Ensure that reading and writing rights are respected.

Mechanisms that make it difficult to modify historical records and make it easy to detect

When someone tries to do it

Where the locks are very different in configuration, and the functionality is whether they are publicly available

Or private; Like any network open to the public, there are

It differs from a private network. Blocking systems have different mechanisms or protocols

Depending on whether they need someone to be able to write to them (public or without permission

Blocks) or if the pool of participants is limited (private or allowed block circuits).

The purpose of the block circuit affects the design of the system. In general, publicly write

Locks are much more limited than private ones.

**How it works**

To be part of the blockchain system, the participating entities will each install and run some

Software that connects their computer or server to other network members. From

By running this software, participants act as separate validators, called network nodes.

A node network manages a database, also known as a block-chain. Nodes are entry points for new data, as well as checking and distributing new data that has been sent to the block chain.

But in a distributed system without a golden source of truth, as the network comes to a consensus or agrees

What data to write on the block? How do you resolve the situation when equivalent people can talk about conflicting things, but there is no boss for arbitration?

The answer is the use of protocols. The block system will have a protocol, that is, pre-agreed rules for the technical and business validity of the data that should be written, and the rule for determining how consensus is achieved.

A block is created by grouping such transactions. These blocks are added in chronological order, in this way, which resembles a chain, hence the name blockchain. The nodes then store these new blocks in the local block chain

Databases on your computer or server.

**How about conflicting data?**

One node can accept two parts of mutually conflicting data. For example, A: "I sell all my shares to Alice", and "B": "I sell all my shares to Bob." Each node will have to leave it and reject it, because they can not both coexist logically.

The intuitive solution is that the nodes act with the priority of time, keeping the first and rejecting the second. However, different nodes can hear messages in different orders. The messages will be distributed, and some part of the network believes that A happened (and B does not), and the rest of the network will believe B what happened (and A is not). The network is in an unstable state.

How is this allowed? Each node is working on its own version of the truth. Whichever node adds the next block, it will distribute its version of events, and all nodes will read it and act on a new "truth".

**What about contradictory blocks?**

Throughout the network, it is possible to simultaneously add two different blocks to different nodes that create a plug in the chain. In this case, there is a "consensus rule" that helps the nodes determine which block they should believe. In bitkoyne this rule is called "the longest chain rule" - each node recognizes the legitimacy of both candidate blocks, and the situation is resolved when the next block is built on one of the rivals. A longer chain becomes part of the de facto block chain.

## Part 2: Potential uses for the blockchain technology

# Chapter 3: The Banking Industry

## Blockchain in Banking: a measured approach

Blockchain is emerging as a potentially disruptive force capable of transforming the financial services industry by making transactions faster, cheaper, more secure and transparent. Here's our foundational view on how the market is taking shape and what banks should consider as they move from ideation and experimentation to pilot deployments.

## Executive Summary

If market noise is a sign, blockchain - the basic technology of crypto-fibers, such as Bitcoin, - is ready to solve many problems facing the banking industry, providing faster, safer and more transparent transactions. Nevertheless, the history of the blockade is one of the unintended consequences. Blockchain, also known as a distributed book, was originally created as a Bitcoin transaction tracking database. It was designed in 2009, to allow individuals and organizations to process transactions without the need for a central bank or other intermediary, using sophisticated algorithms and a consensus to verify transactions. Fast forward 7 years and many startups and the technology created, banks and financial players today rely on the block chain to provide a reliable alternative to systems that depend on intermediaries and third-party transaction verification. Their goal is to use the distributed accounting method of blockchain to create a system that decentralizes trust - a radical departure from existing transaction processing methods - up to significantly reduce all types of transaction fees and reduce processing time.

The disruptive potential of blockchain is widely claimed as equal to the potential of the early commercial Internet. However, the crucial difference is that, although the Internet allows data exchange, the block chain can allow the exchange of value; That is, it can allow users to trade and trade around the world without the need payment processors, custodians and organizations for settlement and reconciliation. Although blockchain is positioned as an open system for processing transactions in the financial system, banks look inward, experimenting with a distributed register approach to create efficiency and a single version of the digital truth. Their goal is to automate processes, reduce data warehouse costs, minimize duplication of data and improve data security. Like Internet and e-commerce, an opento-all blockchain that violates the traditional the financial market can be associated only with the deployment of trial and error within the limited parameters, whether through internal tests or partnerships between actors and start-ups. However, in order to realize the entire blocking potential in the financial system, the banking industry must come together and establish standards that will ensure compatibility.

Nevertheless, the banks that are planning to deploy the block-schemes must answer a number of fundamental questions. For example, given that existing systems are built on reliable obsolete solutions, how do they determine which process will move to the block chain? In addition, given the rapidly changing landscape of the blockhouse, it is critical to develop a sound long-term plan of action (for example, experiment, strategically deploy, and then scale in a logical progression) to ensure a successful transition from a centralized heritage to fully distributed processing of digital transactions.

# BLOCKCHAIN

We believe that key considerations for banks studying the block chain include:

- Identify opportunities for innovation.
- Determination of feasibility and impact on existing System.
- Verification of the evidence of the concept.
- Understanding the regulatory and information security effects.
- Cut-off realization of the block chain:

Open or authorized.

- Planning for transaction scalability.
- Forming partnerships and cross-functional and Interindustry cooperation.

## Blockchain's promise: banking and beyond

Since the first Bitcoin transaction in January 2009, digital crypto currency has become the subject of debate. While banks and regulators mostly feared Bitcoin, the basic technology of the block chain and distributed book began to attract the attention of banks and start-ups by the end of 2013.

The lure of the block chain was his method of checking and tracking transactions. Instead of a reliable third-party or central bank, it relies on a consensus between a peer-to-peer network of computers based on complex algorithms. Instead of storing in one database, transaction blocks with timestamps are stored in all the value chain systems. This elimination of intermediaries and the decentralization of trust have introduced opportunities for creating processes such as transboundary payments, trade and settlements are faster, more reliable and cheaper. The main elements of Blockchain include:

- **Decentralization**: instead of one central body that controls everything within the ecosystem, blockchain distributes control between all peers in the transaction chain, creating a common infrastructure.
- **Digital Signature**: Blockchain allows you to exchange transaction value using unique digital signatures that rely on public keys (decryption code known to everyone on the network) and private keys (codes known only to the owner) to create ownership confirmation.
- **Mining**: a distributed consensus system rewards miners for verifying and verifying transactions and saves them in blocks using strict cryptographic rules.
- **Data integrity**: The use of complex algorithms and consensus among users ensures that transaction data, once agreed, can not be changed. Thus, the data stored in the block chain acts as the only version of the truth for all parties involved, which reduces the risk of fraud.

**Efficiency and cost reduction**

In addition to trade promotion, the blocking and robust chain model can also be applied to non-monetary transactions. Since it eliminates errors and duplication, blockchain is ideal for converting a multitude of digital processes. The main advantages of the block chain are:

- Reduce the calculation time to a few seconds by removing middlemen.
- Replacement of trusted third parties with the access of all participants of the value chain to cloud assets that verify the identity of each party.
- Significant improvements in security in areas such as payments and credit card fraud, through a decentralized record of public transactions, which stores data on each transaction and is continuously checked by miners.
- Reduction of material costs by eliminating expensive private infrastructure.
- Eliminate error handling through real-time transaction tracking without double
- Full automation of transaction processes, from payment through settlement.
- Remove bottlenecks in the documentation caused by duplication.

Risk reduction due to data integrity is ensured by the chronological storage of data enhanced by cryptography. This, in turn, reduces the burden on compliance and reduces the cost of regulation in areas such as knowledge of your customers (KYC).

**Increased competition**

Blockchain can also provide access to markets traditionally dominated by banks and other financial institutions. In the era of modern digital technologies, banks are witnessing an increase in competition from non-bank players in such areas as mobile payments and lending; Blockchain is likely to increase this competition, as this will reduce the technological barriers for non-traditional supporters that are not digitally measurable. Some examples include:

- Allowed block circuits: companies can create blocked blocks that are designed to select customers for a specific purpose. This service is offered by Setl, which created a permit-based accounting system that can move money and assets in real time to calculate market transactions.
- The creator of liquidity: a system based on blockages can allow companies to become market makers and open cash in exchange for completing a cross-border transaction at a lower rate. This can allow non-profit organizations to compete with banks.
- Equity financing: a block-based platform can provide back funding for equity financing using smart contracts.
- Hybrid crediting. Companies can seek funding from peer-to-peer lenders based on the chain. Since such lenders will have lower operating costs than traditional banks, they can

To charge lower interest rates. The DApp LoanCoin credit network is an example of hybrid lending.

For banks, this should be a signal for their playing in these areas, perhaps by creating their versions of these platforms on the blockchain, as non-traditional players equipped with technology

And without compliance, they could quickly penetrate their traditional strongholds.

# BLOCKCHAIN

## New Banking Prospects

It is assumed that Blockchain will create a new set of opportunities for banks that will cooperate with start-ups, studying the niche of business directions. These include:

- Internet of Things (IoT) plus block chain: Intelligent devices can be enabled for performing offline transactions through intelligent Contracts.
- Tracking of health benefits: a system based on blockages can ensure that the nursing allowance is spent exclusively on health care activities. The system can save time spent on reconciliation, after each transaction, helping with direct processing.
- Any trade: the platform can allow exchange of exchange for any underutilized asset (for example, Wi-Fi routers, computer storage, Coupons, etc.) In exchange for a service or product already agreed upon.

## A Rush of Startups and Incumbents

The attractiveness of blockchain (and resulting applications) can be best appreciated by the attention it receives from start-ups and operators, especially in banking and finance. One the estimate puts the number of launches of blockades more than 200, with an average estimate of 4.4 million. USA. Venture capital financing for Bitcoin and blockchain start-ups has reached $ 1 billion in 2015, and some expect that in 2016 the financing of the blocks will cost $ 2.5 billion.

Meanwhile, many top Western and European banks are studying blockchain applications, either cooperating with start-ups, or creating innovative laboratories to test their evidence of the concept. Outstanding for example, a consortium formed by blocking R3, which so far attracted 42 international banks and financial institutions. R3 created a general laboratory block chains for the financial system. Recently, he linked 11 partner banks to a peer-to-peer distributed register and enforced industry standards and protocols to block banking transactions; He will also develop commercial applications for banks and financial institutions. P3 efforts to create industry standards are a small but a significant step towards creating interoperability solutions blockchain in the financial system. Areas of activity of banks and start-ups include cross-border payments, trading activities, storage services and analysis of customer behavior. For example, Santander claims to have identified 20-25 uses, paying particular attention to international payments and prudent contracts. It is reported that Barclays focuses on 45 experiments on internal use, and Citibank created its own version of Bitcoin called Citicoin. In start-up centers devoted to non-financial use cases, a sharp jump is observed, and it is reported that in 2015 several new facilities were received.

The incoming picture suggests that cases of non-financial use exceed financial ones, which indicates that real-world assets may increasingly be associated with blocking and trading.

**Implementing Blockchain**

Despite the increased activity over the past year or so, it is still very early for the blockade. Initiatives of block chains of banks are at different stages of internal testing. Changes caused by the block chain, such as storing data in several places, rather than in one central location, represent a radical shift in the functioning of banks. This in itself, it can become a serious obstacle to overcoming in terms of organizational culture. Nevertheless, given its destructive potential, it would be unreasonable for banks not to start taking steps to incorporate the blockade into their existing systems.

Below follows a subset of the key initial steps that banks should consider when implementing the blockchain platform together with existing systems.

- Identify opportunities for innovation. The key question that must be asked before the start of the trial is the processes that need to be moved to the block chain. It can be difficult. Blockchain is essentially a common database, and banks typically use database management technologies.
- To store and control access to data. The creation of a working group that explores the pros and cons of moving a process to a block chain will be an ideal place to start. Such a group will function as a start-up and explore areas where a blockchain can add value while remaining in sync with the bank's strategic goals.
- Assess the feasibility and impact on existing systems. This includes weighing the benefits and costs of moving the process for blocking.

Taking into account the influence of key stakeholders and partners movement is critical.

**Test proof of the concept. Not all ideas will have the potential for**

At this point, but once the proof-of-concept (PoC) application is ready, it needs to be tested against real-world simulations to identify areas of improvement. Measuring the results against expectations, banks will be able to refine the application and use this knowledge to develop future applications.

- Understand the regulatory environment and data security. External factors, such as rules, play an important role in the era of the blockchain. The current regulatory framework does not contain provisions on the use of technology that could eliminate intermediaries. Saving customer data on computers in

  Different countries will also require banks to comply with data privacy laws that may vary from country to country.

Similarly, there is no framework for rules that allow contracts on capital markets to be concluded, as they exist today. While regulators will eventually develop, it will be important for the

Early engines to introduce this factor into their long-term plans.

- Determine the nature of the implementation of the chain of blocks: open or allowed. It is known that most banks are working on closed / Allowed blocking platforms. Given the embryonic state of the technology, it is reasonable for them to maintain control, which means that the central administrator authorizes participation in the block chain. However, all the advantages of decentralization, such as a reduction in transaction costs, can not be achieved without giving up control. This block-chain approach makes sense in the short term, but as the platforms come out on their own, players in the industry will be pressured to realize the real benefits of the blockchain platform.

- Calculate scalability. The Bitcoin community continues to discuss the best way to increase the processing efficiency of transaction processing from the chain of blocks from the current seven transactions for Secondly, since real scenarios will require banks to process thousands of transactions per second. The proposed solutions include increasing the block size limit from the current 1 MB per block, direct payments channels between two users and centralized servers that process transactions with an indirect chain.

Looking forward: partnership and cooperation

Among all activities related to the block chain, we believe that the "wait and see" approach will be suboptimal. Banks need to start with

By creating plans that allow blockchain technologies to coexist with their inherited run-the-bank systems. Blockchain must mature and become sufficiently reliable to replace existing banking systems. The key to unlocking the potential of blockages in the long term is a common protocol that ensures interoperability. Although visibility is hazy

On this front, banks planning to move their processes to the block chain should begin by assessing how interoperability can advance their chain goals.

It's time to start experimenting, and to this end, banks are inclined to approach that combines internal testing with participation in consortia, including related banks and technology providers to investigate the use of the chain. These experiments will lay the groundwork - in the form of protocols and standards - on which will be built in the future of the block chain. Leaders such as R3, Hyperledger Project, Post Trade Distributed Ledger (PTDL) and Digital Asset Holding create a safe space for conducting pilot tests for prototype blocks. It is important to note that financial institutions and technology providers can feed on each other's ideas and experiments while simultaneously identifying areas of focus and avoidance. This will allow banks to identify and create key skills and use collective knowledge to create a plan that will facilitate a seemingly inevitable transition to a future based on a chain.

## Chapter 4: Examples of public and private concepts Blockchain

There was a huge interest in blockchain, the technology on which bitcoin functions. Nakamoto developed the blockade as an acceptable solution to the game theory puzzle - the task of the Byzantine general. This leads to the fact that a number of firms use technology in different ways to solve real-world problems, wherever there is an element of trust. Most of them can be associated with the possibility of providing evidence of possession - for documents, program modules / licenses, voting, etc.

As you know, we at LTP have done a lot of research to understand other options for using block systems, in addition to bitcoat-based payments. Recently, we released a comprehensive analysis of 50+ start-ups and 20 cases of blocking use. Although there were news of large companies hosting bitcoins (for example: Amazon, Microsoft, Dell) and the general recognition reaching the figure of 100,000+, with deeper consideration we understand that large corporations do not store Bitcoin payments. They usually work with the Bitcoin payment processor, which converts bitcoins into cash when and when they receive payment, and this converted amount is what corporate parties take to their account. What a bummer!

By definition, blockchain is the register of all transactions that have been performed, and can be considered as a platform for writing, and transactions that are executed after execution can not be changed later. This platform was further divided into Public and Private blockchain. Is there a third? A hybrid mode, such as the "consortium block chain", presented by Vitalik Butterin, founder of Ethereum, a decentralized Web platform for publication 3.0.

**Public Blockchain**

A public block chain is a platform on which any person on the platform can read or write to the platform if they can show proof of work for the same. In this space there was a lot of activity, because the number of potential users that can generate any technology in this space is great. In addition, public blockade is considered to be completely decentralized to block purposes. Here are some examples:

Ethereum, a provider of a decentralized platform and programming language that helps to run intelligent contracts and allows developers to publish distributed applications.

Factom, a record management provider, recording business processes for business and governments.

Blockstream, a technology provider of side chains, is focused on expanding the capabilities of Bitcoin. The company began experimenting with the provision of accounting (considered a function performed on private block circuits) using publicchchain technology.

**Private blockchain**

On the other hand, the private blockchain only grants the owner the right to any changes that need to be made. This can be seen as a similar version of the existing infrastructure in which the owner (the centralized authority) has the right to change the rules, return transactions, etc., based on the need. This can be a concept with

## BLOCKCHAIN

great interest from FI and large companies. He could find use cases to create his own systems and reduce costs, while at the same time increasing their effectiveness. Here are some examples:

Eris Industries, aims to become a provider of a common software database using blockchain technology.

Blockstack, is aimed at providing operations of financial institutions of financial institutions, including clearing and settlements on a private block block.

Multichain, a provider of a distributed open source database for financial transactions.

Chain Inc., provider of blockchain APIs. Chain is partnering with Nasdaq OMX Group Inc. to provide a platform that allows the trading of a private joint stock company with a block chain.

Let's look at whether there is a hybrid blockhouse concept (the third type). The block-chain of the consortium will be a combination of both public and private. While the ability to read and write can be expanded to a certain number of people / nodes. This can be used by groups of organizations / firms that come together, work on developing different models, cooperating with each other. Consequently, they can receive a lock with limited access, work on their decisions and support intellectual property rights in the consortium.

**Advantages of Public blockchains Systems**

Public block circuits, including Bitcoin, Ethereum, Hyperledger and most Altcons, are designed to be accessible to anyone who has the appropriate technology that until now meant a computer and Internet access.

Ripple is technically a public block key, but it is an interesting outstanding because it is built with public architecture, but it is privately controlled through a centralized ownership of the base currency and the software with closed source code. Whatever the benefits of decentralization, they are mostly lost because of a closed nature that can be used to harm the network at any time when Ripple Labs own company Herself makes any changes.

All data on public block circuits is public by default, although it is usually conceivable to hide the actual identity of all related participants, as Bitcoin does. This openness has advantages that never existed before, such as the ability to withstand hacking or capital management from repressive regimes. They provide their security with their "publicity", where each participant can see all the balances on the accounts and the movement of all transactions. This method still seems strange to us, because we are so new to this approach to security, but in the seven years of bitcoine existence no one has found a way to overcome this safety in practice. Unfortunately, the cost is not always worth the benefits. To organize such a network, it is necessary to reduce the capacity between the parties. Less data will move more slowly across the network, as they must be duplicated by all parties.

Meanwhile, private locks are protected by an ancient model of user rights and secrets, with which we have become so comfortable since the first lock was invented. The less people know about your database, the more secure it is in this model. This can work fine if you do not plan to share it with many people, but throughout history there have been many examples of this approach to failing security. The keys can be designed to be very smart, but there is always a hacker who is smarter. (Or an inner guy who is modest.)

This applies not only to the content of the block, but also to the rules governing it. The more private a block-chain is launched, the more likely that the rules governing the block chain can be changed.

While simple user rights management protects private databases, crypto-economy, a mixture of cryptography and economic incentives, it is a method that protects public locks. Because different organizations and users have different goals for their networks, it is unlikely that one method will prevail over another. Both have their own niche, although it is still widely believed that their niches are misunderstood, so the question of their value is the subject of ongoing debate.

**Time will tell about security**

The essence of the problem boils down to the fact that private locks can be sufficiently safe to use in large volumes. No hacker is going to attack your blockade if it is only used for bingo nights in a retirement home. However, at the moment when the world finds out that your blockbuster has millions of dollars of payments flowing through it, you basically just launched the last hackathon, in which there is a multi-million-dollar winning win.

It may seem that public blockers should show themselves more than private networks, but the block-block bitcoin has already been tested under incredible stress. This is the only one proven and protected from such hacking, with a seven-year history that is too strong for any hacker to win, despite the day of paying a salary of 6.7 billion dollars for it. The allowed block-schemes simply can not assert that they are well protected.

It is for this reason that Paul Chow, the bitlocked adviser to the US Commodity Futures and Commodity Futures Commission (CFTC), talks very little about non-bitcock-block chains. "Many proposals for the use of blockless without bitkoyan are extremely erroneous," Zhou said in an interview with the New York Business Journal. "Perhaps incredibly wrong, and, of course, not proven." Chow is a former merchant trader at Goldman Sachs and is currently the CEO of LedgerX, a block-start-up with an office in New York on Madison Avenue. He spends his days creating what he hopes will become the "first federal regulation of Bikoyne options and a clearing house to list and clean up fully secured, physically grounded bitocone options for the institutional market" when he is not in the center, advising the CFTC on Bitkoyne to Their offices.

**Maximum maximum blockchains**

This mentality, especially optimistic over long-term prospects, is very common among early adopters of bitcoins and those who are attracted to bitcoins from an economic point of view. This is called "Bitcoin maximalism", which is the term coined by the creator of the Etherium, Vitalik Buterin. He argues that the bitlock-block chain will ultimately be the only dominant, safe blockbuster in the long run, squeezing the rest, and ultimately all other currencies.

This position is based both on informatics and on economics. In each of these, the concept known as the Network Effect is extremely effective for the first engine in a new network or protocol, and it never stops crowding out competitors. Regardless of whether the maximalists of bitcoins are right, applying them to bitcoins or just being naive, they will be revealed in time, but it is clear that public blockmics offer unique advantages that private blockages simply can not.

# BLOCKCHAIN

## Advantages unique to public blockchains

For example, public blockchain is a transparency mechanism. In Vitalik Buterina's blog "On Public and Private Block Chains" written last August, he noted that public locks "protect application users from developers" by establishing that there are certain things that even application developers do not have the authority to do " A good example of this is a social network user or some other member site where an owner changing their rules can create difficulties or losses for users.Luckily, whenever facebook makes a change They inform the public and only the affected people leave the service.However, if they were not open and honest in their changes, it would be useful for users to require that a public lock base their rules.

Buterin also mentions that when several organizations use the same block-chain, its growth benefits from the effect of the network. This will not only increase the popularity and, therefore, the usefulness of several organizations contributing to its development, but can also reduce transaction costs. "If we have a system of domain names on the block chain and the currency on the same chain," explained Buterin, "then we can cut costs down to zero with the help of a smart contract."

There are other, smaller advantages for public blockades, but one powerful argument against private locks sticks out. The presentation, popularized by the most popular reporter on bitkonam Andreas Antonopoulos, makes a comparison between private blockbusters and corporate intranets. In the next video, thoughtfully entitled "Bubble boy and the sewer rat" (hint: bitcoin is a rat, but it's good). Antonopoulos argues that private locks are, in fact, used today in the business world, but they have the same limitations as corporate networks of the company, including significant security problems.

The main conclusion is that allowed locks create an environment in which malware has the advantage, so security problems are permanent, and sometimes completely eliminate your network. Antonopoly is in strong agreement with Zhou, that the sharing of value between different entities still needs a public block-chain, and today it means blocking Bitcoin.

**Advantages of private blockchains**

Meanwhile, there are certain advantages for private blockages that should not be overlooked in certain situations. First of all, the transaction rate of a private block chain can be faster than any other blockchain solution, even approaching the speed of a normal database, which is not a block chain. This is due to the fact that there are several nodes with a high level of trust. You do not need every node to check the transaction, in fact, all of them are mostly trusted, so there is no need to perform all the thorough work.

Confidentiality, obviously, is more guaranteed for a private blockchain. This makes the privacy policy for the data in this block-chain exactly the same as if it were in another database; Without the need to have access to access permissions and do everything the old way, but at least the data is not publicly available to anyone who has a network connection.

Private blockchain can either have completely free, or at least very low-cost transactions. If one organization monitors and processes all transactions, then they do not need to charge for their work. However, even if transaction processing is performed by several organizations, such as competing banks, for example, transaction fees can be very small for the same reasons that they can be so fast; A complete agreement between the nodes is not required, so a smaller number of nodes must perform work for any transaction.

Finally, and perhaps most importantly in the current conditions of banks that cover private locks, it is so easy that choosing a private block can help protect their main product from failures. Banks and governments are interested in seeing their product, the national currency of the exchange rate that they trade remains valuable. Since the best use of a public block chain is to provide a new, non-national currency such as bitcoyne, it represents a devastating threat to their main stream of profit or organization, and these companies should be avoided at all costs.

**Private blockchain come in order**

There are already much more private locks than anyone can track, thanks to companies such as Rubix Deloitte, Eris Industries and Streamcore from AlphaPoint, who all sell ready-made solutions for private block chains directly for business. There is also Microsoft, which started offering "Blockchain as a service" (BaaS) or private nodes of the blockages, packaged as "quick templates" in Azure cloud service. Deploying these block nodes, both public and private, is extremely simple for Azure members, so now it is possible to test the lock and eject it in an hour. Finally, there is a desktop, the deployment of a private blockchain system on your desktop computer, even in a Windows environment, with Multichain. This allows you to quickly develop, deploy and manage private block circuits in accordance with your specifications.

However, large, institutionalized projects, such as the R3 CEV, the upcoming Consortium block chain or its own SWIFT solution, receive all the press and fame, even though they are not yet completed. If blockchain maximalists are wrong in that Bitcoin becomes a global monetary standard, it is likely that one of these top-level bank consortiums using private blockchain will dominate the future of basic finance.

## Chapter 5: Financial Services - The Blockchain Innovation

Understanding what kind of development the blockchain falls into is the initial step for a productive utilizing of the innovation. So how about we do a smidgen of the hypothesis.

The blockchain development is a radical, fitness obliterating advancement in that the oddity of the innovation would render the present one out of date, and it is likewise a troublesome, compositional advancement in that its execution advertise wide would prompt a rearrangement of plans of action of any industry and its on-screen characters.

**Radical Innovation versus Incremental Innovation**

Rather than an incremental advancement, which manages the change of a current item, administration or process, a radical development concerns the effect of the advancement available in which the association works? It is measured by the interruption it makes, which means the requirement for absolutely new assembling or administration procedures to have the capacity to utilize this advancement.

Gary Pisano[i] makes a further refinement between radical advancement and troublesome development. He clarifies that, while a radical advancement requires a mechanical achievement however not another plan of action, a troublesome development is an inverse.

By evacuating the requirement for agents, the Blockchain innovation can totally reshape any industry and specifically the capital markets, essentially affecting existing plans of action. In any case, before it is received broad, issues, for example, interoperability and adaptability must be settled. Those difficulties will permit the making of new instruments that will frame a radical new biological system.

## Skill Enhancing Innovation versus Competence-Destroying Innovation

An advancement is said to be capability improving when it develops on a current innovation utilizing company's current abilities.

In actuality, an advancement is said to be skill wrecking when it replaces an innovation and in this manner render association's abilities out of date. It is typically the instance of radical developments.

Schumpeter[ii] expounded on the Creative Destruction, which he portrayed as a 'procedure of modern change that ceaselessly upsets the monetary structure from inside, perpetually obliterating the old one, unendingly making another one.' To a specific degree, the blockchain innovation can be contrasted with this idea inside capital markets. On the off chance that it is embraced by officeholders, the center and back workplaces work as we probably are aware them today could wind up noticeably outdated.

## Compositional Innovation versus Component Innovation

Each question, item, framework or process is made of individual parts that connect and are connected. In his work on the many-sided quality of things, Simon[iii] exhibited that each element is an arrangement of segments and every segment is likewise an arrangement of segments et cetera until there is just the rudimentary molecule left.

The part development, likewise called secluded advancement, influences one or a few segments of the innovation, however, does not adjust the general design of the framework.

The engineering development either changes the entire way the framework works or influences the way segments associate together. Building development all the time deduces part advancement as it requires both changes in the fundamental segments and subsequently, changes in the way they relate[IV]. Subsequently, a structural advancement consolidates mechanical and plan of action interruptions. The Distributed Ledger Technology can be delegated a building advancement as it will change the design of exchange forms by evacuating the requirements for some counterparties included – or if nothing else by changing the parts they as of now have.

**Worldwide blockchain advancement: U.S. slacks, Europe and China lead**

Nobody can foresee the eventual fate of blockchain similarly we couldn't anticipate the fate of the Internet in the mid-'90s. In any case, it is clear this innovation will have a huge effect.

From partnerships with new companies and governments to associations, the race is on to take advantage of the idea of appropriated and decentralized trust with a specific end goal to decrease grinding and manufacture more legitimate, straightforward, and effective structures for business and administration.

The U.S. has been to some degree calm on the blockchain startup front, which has more to do with administrative issues than an absence of organizations that can improve, and that has brought about a nonattendance of blockchain buzz in Silicon Valley. Kraken and Coinbase are both in the Bay Area, however, are digital currency driven, and there's a genuine lack of U.S.- construct blockchain new companies working on ventures in wellbeing, vitality, protection, store network, and some alternate verticals that are being investigated in different nations.

Despite the fact that a fourth of all worldwide blockchain organizations on Outlier Ventures' splendid blockchain tracker is from the U.S., they are cryptographic money or bitcoin-centered; few are tapping blockchain's colossal potential for non-cash purposes.

New York is the epicenter of the American blockchain group, basically, because the money related industry is scrambling to make sense of how to manage the genuine danger, it is confronting with dispersed record innovation. In any case, New York is additionally home to several major players outside fund: Consensys is the fundamental player on the worldwide Ethereum organizes pushing blockchain past managing an account. Furthermore, Digital Asset Holdings has raised more than $70 million from 15 of the world's biggest innovation and budgetary firms to fabricate secure and dispersed preparing instruments to accelerate settlement, diminish expenses, and upgrade security and straightforwardness in directed enterprises. Chief Blythe Masters, a financial expert and previous official at JPMorgan Chase, turned down an occupation to run Barclay's speculation division to construct the organization.

# BLOCKCHAIN

**SEC puts breaks on U.S. biological community**

Be that as it may the blockchain biological community in America is moving gradually. The U.S. Securities and Exchange Commission has set up a noteworthy detour to development by not tending to the new wonder of Initial Coin Offerings (ICOs) and giving no administrative system to them to exist, accordingly stagnating U.S. blockchain improvements.

While Singapore and Switzerland are beginning to swing open the entryways as the main two locales on the planet where tokens are dealt with as a benefit and not as a security, the SEC is dragging its heels, which is bad for American pioneers who need to raise stores utilizing these one of a kind money related instruments or for Europeans and Asians who need to open up to U.S. financial specialists.

Some European ICOs are even IP-blocking Americans from partaking because of the potential legitimate ramifications; and that is not incredible for American speculators. In any case, American Brock Pierce and his VC group from Blockchain Capital as of late chosen to take a risk at disturbing their industry by doing their own particular ICO — the world's first KYC AML consistent crowd sale. Puncture raised 20 percent of his association's next reserve by pitching advanced tokens to speculators a week ago, pulling in $10 million in six hours.

Be that as it may, it was difficult. He needed to consolidate the substance doing the ICO in Singapore and utilize Regulation S and D exceptions with the SEC keeping in mind the end goal to raise cash from universal financial specialists and also household speculators. For the U.S., that constrained the raise to a minor 99 to certify American financial specialists, while whatever remains of the world could contribute as much as it needed.

"It's my conviction that in the following 10 or 20 years, no startup on the planet will be financed in any capacity other than as a token," Pierce disclosed to American Banker.

Fortunately no less than eight states are chipping away at blockchain enactment advancing the utilization of bitcoin and blockchain innovation, which is promising. Be that as it may, on the government level, no bills have been submitted.

### Canada demonstrates more blockchain cordial

Canada has a dynamic blockchain startup group for the most part because of the way that Ethereum exuded from the Toronto bitcoin group and there is a bunch of ability brought together in the nation's biggest city, beginning with Vitalik Buterin, who is the mind behind Ethereum. Also, William Mougayar and Don Tapscott, two of the most unmistakable creators in the blockchain space are likewise out of Canada. What's more, not at all like the U.S. SEC, which has been tranquil, the Canadian Securities Administrators (CSA) have been more proactive by propelling another fintech "sandbox" program gone for blockchain new companies and different firms working with monetary innovation.

### China effectively encourages blockchain appropriation

Making sense of what is happening in China is constantly confounded when you are looking in all things considered. As indicated by Jane Zhang from Skyledger, situated in Shanghai, the legislature is adopting a tolerant strategy. Zhang, a power player in the Chinese blockchain group, says they are savvy enough to know the following huge thing.

In a current meeting, she said that a portion of the bitcoin trades are notwithstanding loaning without a managing an account permit, which, she says, demonstrates the Chinese government is more inspired by ensuring advancement than whatever else.

The focal government is putting monstrous venture into a portion of the poorer areas in China and are wanting to manufacture blockchain parks to allure a portion of the top blockchain minds comprehensively to come to China upheld with huge subsidizing," said Zhang. "There is significantly more blockchain new companies this year than a year ago.

Her particular group at Skyledger comprises of a world class worldwide gathering of blockchain designers, numerous from Eastern Europe, who have moved over to Shanghai to deal with her private blockchain stage, which was quite recently picked by the Dubai government for Customs and Immigration.

The Chinese market has seen a whirlwind of advancements over the previous year with the development of consortia, for example,

- China Ledger Alliance: Comprises territorial trades to make an open source blockchain convention to help a possible 'Web of Everything' for China.
- Financial Blockchain Shenzhen Consortium: Have individuals that incorporate Ping An Insurance (some portion of R3, a worldwide consortium of more than 50 monetary organizations required in R&D for blockchain utilization) and a Tencent auxiliary. This consortium plans

to work together on research and gathering wide blockchain ventures, with an emphasis on capital markets innovation, securities trade, exchanging stages, keeping the money, and disaster protection. It intends to make securities exchanging stage model and create credit, computerized resource registry, and receipt administration administrations.

- Qianhai International Blockchain Ecosphere Alliance: Aims to build up a proficient biological community for creating blockchain innovation and its applications by consolidating terrain China and universal ability, innovation, and capital. The Alliance, which incorporates Microsoft, IBM, and Hong Kong's Applied Science and Technology Research Institute (ASTRI), plans to quicken the commercialization of blockchain R&D and elevate its application to help China's social and monetary improvement

**Australia, New Zealand try things out**

Furthermore, not to forget Antipodea, Australia's Central Bank is leading inward blockchain research and China behemoth Alibaba is utilizing blockchain to battle China's fake sustenance, with a store network extend being trialed in New Zealand and Australia.

**Europe in the number one spot**

Europe from multiple points of view has driven the blockchain surge. The eminent open source culture that penetrates the mainland loans itself well to the new unique of blockchain, and both private and open elements are effectively required in blockchain ventures.

# BLOCKCHAIN

What's more, indeed, the lion's share of ICOs are currenting being directed by European blockchain new businesses — numerous from Eastern Europe.

As far as blockchain center points, the fundamental centralizations of new companies are in London, Amsterdam, Barcelona, Berlin, and Switzerland's Cryptovalley.

Estonia's Guardtime is not just working with its own particular government to utilize blockchain for wellbeing records however has likewise contracted with associations, for example, NATO. Furthermore, America's Nasdaq has connected with the modest nation in the Baltics to create applications. Skype prime supporter Jaan Tallinn has likewise commenced a blockchain startup commercial center situated in Estonia called Funderbeam.

The United Kingdom's main researcher, Sir Mark Walport, unleashed a monstrous 88-page blockchain report in January, delineating the capability of blockchain and demonstrating how it can change the conveyance of open administrations and lift profitability in government. Before long, GovCoin Systems Limited, a London-headquartered monetary innovation organization, reported blockchain trials to help government points in streamlining the dispersion of welfare benefits.

The Isle of Man government has started to utilize a blockchain registry to record which organizations on the Isle of Man are dynamic in utilizing the arrangement of dispersed online records.

Bank Of England Governor Mark Carney expressed not long ago that the BoE is investigating the approach and specialized issues postured by Central Bank Digital Currencies (CBDC) and creating blockchain verification of-ideas.

The Netherlands' ING Bank finished an astounding 27 blockchain Proof of Concepts (POCs) by February, and Dutch saving money mammoth Rabobank has additionally been exceptionally dynamic. Worldwide wellbeing mammoth Philips was well in front of the pack, investigating blockchain for wellbeing in mid 2016. Also, the Dutch Central Bank did an undeniable bitcoin clone explore different avenues regarding something many refer to as DNBcoin and is pushing ahead with more tests.

The Danish Central Bank is considerably more diversion with arrangements to in the end issue blockchain-based E-krone as its save money. What's more, the French Central bank is likewise trying blockchain.

Sweden is prepared to move into arrive rights with an open private push to record arrive titles on a Blockchain that started in March.

Brussels as of late proposed a blockchain pilot to look at administrative issues as the official branch of the European Union needs to make a blockchain confirmation of-idea concentrated on control.

Despite the fact that the lawful angles have not been dealt with at the EU level, Switzerland is fashioning the way. In April, Swiss administrative body FINMA declared its steady position for another authorizing classification for money related pioneers doing some saving money exercises, however with constrained acknowledgment of customer resources and no loaning movement. Contrasted with a full bank, the authorizing prerequisites would be

# BLOCKCHAIN

less broad in light of the fact that the dangers are lower and the extent of business is restricted.

In this manner, it's no big surprise that the 30 km vale amongst Zug and Zurich has been authored Cryptovalley and is viewed as the focal point of the blockchain startup biological system all inclusive.

**Who will move speediest?**

The following couple of years will be fascinating as blockchain keeps on picking up footing and makes both dangers and chances to existing plans of action. The inquiry is: Who will improve quickest with this innovation? It's open to question now, however unmistakably ICOs will affect the biological community in the short to medium term; and much will rely on upon the controllers who have the ability to stop or free up the new liquidity being made by means of ICOs, which will give the fuel to the up and coming era of blockchain advancement.

## Chapter 6: Blockchain Uses - Financial and Non-Financial

When we distributed the business' first infographic/cover the different non-money related utilize instances of the blockchain, the reaction for it was phenomenal with a large number of site visits, a huge number of social offers and various inquiries being sent to us. Much obliged for such a mind-boggling reaction. This is our third refresh to give a far-reaching photo of the different applications that are being investigated with blockchain.

It is presently a well-established certainty that the utilization instances of blockchain have been expanding by the day. There has Increasingly been an expansive number of routes in which genuine resources could be connected to the blockchain and exchanged carefully. A proof-of-idea is being kept running for exchanging items (like physical bars of gold, silver and precious stone) after being verified through blockchain, building up responsibility for bequest properties, to give race voting, and so on.

Aside from new businesses, banks additionally have been effectively putting resources into this decentralized framework as we have appeared in the course of events. Different banks have demonstrated premium and began exploring different avenues regarding the blockchain.

The beneath infographic gives a depiction of organizations and the wide applications that they are giving over blockchain. These incorporate both non-budgetary and money related/cash related (bitcoin and other advanced monetary forms) applications.

## Chapter 7: Role of blockchain technology in future capital markets

Interest in blockchain for capital markets has detonated lately, with interest in this developing innovation dramatically increasing in the vicinity of 2014 and 2015 alone. Following Accenture's current speculation and union with Digital Asset Holdings, we examine how and why blockchain-empowered circulated records are ready to change venture managing an account in the coming years.

**Why would that be the ideal time for blockchain innovation in capital markets?**

Over the most recent 20 years, we've seen noteworthy innovative progressions in capital markets, a lot of it moved in front-office capacities. Center and back-office capacities, then again, frequently stayed moderate and wasteful. A benefit can be exchanged today electronically in barely a second and afterward take days to settle. Both venture banks and their customers are requesting more — and the market is reacting.

Interest in blockchain innovation expanded from $30 million in 2014 to $75 million in 2015, and is relied upon to develop in 2016 and past. Activities like the Linux Hyperledger Project are endeavoring to create open-source circulated record structures with the goal that designers can concentrate on building industry applications. In the interim, consortiums like the Linux Foundation are uniting innovation and capital markets firms to set up norms for blockchain innovation in capital markets. There's most likely about it: Change is brewing.

ADRIAN COOPER

**Will blockchain innovation supplant the capital markets environment as we probably am aware it?**

The feasible result is that blockchain innovation will basically work inside the current foundation or biological community to rebuild and rearrange many existing procedures and strip out critical wasteful aspects related with compromise. Banks will be searching for approaches to end up noticeably more proficient and enhance customer administrations, and controllers will be occupied with expanding straightforwardness and upgrading execution and settlement.

**How do "brilliant contracts" fit into the photo?**

"Brilliant contracts" are installed with PC conventions that can naturally check and execute the terms of the agreement without depending on an incorporated business rationale motor. The advocates of "savvy contract" arrangements normally imagine expelling middle people through their answers for accomplish more prominent effectiveness while keeping up auditability of the exchanges. While it appears to be likely that individual exchanges can be effectively empowered through this innovation, there are as yet specialized difficulties to be worked out as to what happens when it turns out badly, for example, information sustain issues, upstream security issues, execution time periods, and so on.

Be that as it may, it is the suggestions on the general framework that raise considerably more genuine concerns. An essential capacity of delegates (e.g., clearinghouses) is to guarantee that on the off chance that one counterparty can't satisfy their piece of an exchange, that the others can be kept entire and systemic hazard diminished. The capacity for a "shrewd contract" based answer for give a similar level of hazard alleviation is not yet clear, and would be required to make controllers agreeable.

Interestingly, the probability of clearinghouses to execute an alternate sort of blockchain answer for increment effectiveness, auditability and straightforwardness appears to be more probable and would protect the present foundation, front-to-reverses and administrative develops.

Brilliant contracts might be a practical approach later on, yet until further notice, it appears to be judicious to keep on managing a united arrangement of tenets and builds halfway, and exploit "message" based disseminated record and blockchain answers for accomplish the focused on productivity, control and straightforwardness picks up.

Accenture as of late shaped a union with Digital Asset Holdings, a circulated record innovation designer. Enlighten us regarding that choice.

We trust that blockchain innovations — and blockchain-empowered dispersed records specifically — can possibly change capital markets and the budgetary administrations scene. So when the open door emerged to collaborate with one of the rising pioneers in the field, we didn't reconsider.

In January, Accenture and 12 different associations from over the worldwide budgetary environment pooled assets to put more than $60 million in Digital Asset Holdings. We likewise framed a cooperation with the gathering to work together on creative answers for banks, financiers and foundation suppliers that Accenture will execute as a favored frameworks integrator. We are sure that this current organization's product is going to fundamentally enhance post-exchange preparing, making it more secure and more effective while lessening costs and opening new income open doors for venture banks.

**How is Accenture Technology Labs supporting blockchain improvement?**

Accenture's Technology Lab in Sophia Antipolis fills in as our Blockchain Center of Excellence and positions Accenture as a key and dynamic player in the blockchain space. It gives access to both specialized and business skill around blockchain. The middle concentrates on building perspectives, evidence of ideas, instructive materials and the sky is the limit from there. It addresses all the conveyed record capacities crosswise over various blockchain plans (open, consortium and private), with industry verticalization and area specialization (IoT, exchanges, informing, and so on.), supported by the best fundamental advancements from new businesses, our key accomplices and from the open group.

In particular, the Labs give reference architecture(s), specialized combination modules and structures, industry particular utilize cases and preparing materials. It gives the fundamental due perseverance and testing of innovation applications with our underlying innovation accomplices and arrangement suppliers, for example, Digital Asset Holdings, IBM, Ripple, Eris and Multichain, and also testing of developing outsider arrangement suppliers which gives it an interesting capacity to write about market patterns and blockchain new businesses. To date, the Labs have constructed various working blockchain arrangements in sandbox situations, taking into consideration profound testing abilities in front of generation prepared arrangements.

# BLOCKCHAIN

## Quite a while from now, where do you see blockchain innovation in capital markets?

Blockchain arrangements won't supplant the present capital markets biological community. Rather, we trust this innovation will offer the chance to on a very basic level re-engineer processes- driving blockchain from experimentation to standard reception over various business applications. These procedures incorporate ones which are at present hard to accommodate inferable from various inside and additionally outer members, inactivity difficulties and security concerns. Cases incorporate settlement advancement, customer onboarding KYC/AML, standard settlement directions, guarantee administration, administrative review and detailing, and a large group of others.

5 blockchain applications for capital markets

- Slowly yet definitely blockchain applications are being tried in capital markets.
- For the innovation to grab hold, a discount change to the foundation and esteem chain is required.

Circulated Ledger Technology may can possibly change a large number of the procedures in budgetary markets. The innovation guarantees speed, security and much lower IT costs.

In any case, for the innovation to grab hold, a discount change to the current monetary administrations foundation and esteem chain will be required, takes note of a current report by Celent and Misys that investigated the utilization instances of DLT for capital markets. Relatively few utilize cases have moved past the confirmation of idea, yet the pilots and ventures that are en route demonstrate the capability of the beginning innovation.

**Credit subordinates**

Credit subordinates exchange advance hazard to an outsider. This is an immense market. As per the Bank of International Settlements, worldwide OTC subsidiaries came to $544,052 billion of notional sum remarkable. This market has an extremely complex post exchange forms that will profit by cost decreases and efficiencies from effective usage of DLT.

In April 2016, a working gathering including Bank of America Merrill Lynch, Citi, Credit Suisse, JP Morgan, the DTCC, Axoni and Markit reported it had effectively tried a permissioned, conveyed P2P organize for single-name credit default swaps. The exchange utilized shrewd contacts to oversee terms and occasion preparing.

**Money values clearing**

Utilizing DLT for clearing and settlement can quicken the settlement cycles and advance administration of capital and hazard. In January 2016, the Australian Securities Exchange reported it will work with Digital Asset Holding to outline another post-exchange arrangement in light of DLT for the Australian value showcase.

**Repurchase assentions**

Repurchase assentions, where one side pitches a security to another with a consent to get it back later, assumes a significant part in giving liquidity to capital markets. The present procedure incorporates arranging and settling the buy however between merchant specialists and the Fixed Income Clearing Corporation in a 2 stage approach, which is both exorbitant and tedious.

Utilizing DTL framework would guarantee merchant classification, diminish inertness, operational hazard, and general settlement commitments.

In walk 2016, the DTCC reported a proof of idea DLT answer for deal with the clearing and settlement of U.S. Treasury, Agency, and Agency Mortgage-Backed repurchase assention exchanges.

**Syndicated credits**

A syndicated credit is an advance subsidized from numerous moneylenders and is intended to improve the advance procedure instead of have various respective advances. Different sorts of credits can be gathered together in one syndicated advance understanding. Likewise, such credits can be sold to different gatherings. A specialist bank is selected by the moneylenders to direct the advance, which is a huge errand that incorporates figurings of distributions and compromises, development of task of proprietorship and understanding modifications.

Applying DLT can help robotize the part of the operator, and in addition monitor the full chain of responsibility for credits.

Ipreo and Symbiont declared they are incorporating Ipreo's advance settlement stage and Symbiont's shrewd contracts to convey completely computerized settlement and support for syndicated credits.

**Privately owned business securities**

Overseeing value in private securities incorporates many procedures that will profit by DLT, including financial specialist organization, documentation and offering value in optional markets. DLT can help with enhanced levels of straightforwardness, consistence, and trust.

In December 2015, NASDAQ declared that Chain could utilize its Nasdaq Linq blockchain record innovation to effectively total and record a private securities exchange. NASDAQ expressed this decreased settlement time and wiped out the requirement for paper stock testaments.

BNP Paribas is outlining a pilot conspire with SmartAngels allowing privately owned businesses to issue securities on an essential market with e-authentications and access to an optional market by means of blockchain innovation.

# Chapter 8: Blockchain applications

This present day web manages resources, your most significant quick things that you can touch and need to ensure. These benefits are put away in encoded shape on a system to-organize chain called the blockchain or record, where every member sees who you work with. This not just ensures your business dealings and forestalls burglary, be that as it may, likewise, improves your undertakings, stimulates the procedure, diminishes blunders, and spares you from enlisting an outsider.

This decentralized blockchain framework will change your life from the way you execute business or oversee resources, to the way you utilize your machines, vote, lease an auto, and even demonstrate your identity. En route, it will change banks and other money related organizations, healing facilities, organizations, and governments among others.

This is what the blockchain does and what it intends to you.

**Blockchain Finance**

**Decentralized cryptographic forms of money.**

At its least complex, cryptographic forms of money, or advanced coins, will be coins that are gone through an electronic system. You can make exchanges with check, wiring, or money. You can likewise utilize a kind of virtual cash, most broadly Bitcoin (BTC) additionally Litecoin, Peercoin, or Dogecoin, among others, where you utilize an electronic coded deliver to make the exchange.

The more profitable the exchange, the more you need to secure it. Customary frameworks enlist an arbiter, for example, a financier or a settlement organization to guarantee trust. Islanders of Yap had an alternate arrangement. They kept a mental record of who possessed what and alluded to this disseminated group record when question emerged. The blockchain is this group record on a more extensive, advanced scale. It stretches out over the globe, with PC clients from Yemen, Rome, Vermont et cetera where every hub in the system records and checks the information of every exchange that happens inside the system. Records are changeless, complete and open – which is the reason clients adore the blockchain for finagling sketchy or dangerous exchanges.

**How it functions**

Every exchange is an advanced "piece" that should be checked before it's permitted to enter the framework.

**Inquiries include:**

- Is the cash there?
- Are sender and recipient respectable?
- Is the demand honest to goodness? Et cetera.

Every PC on the system contends on unscrambling the appropriate responses, and the triumphant PC includes this "square" to the "blockchain" in the request that the "piece" arrived. The champ communicates his evidence to whatever is left of the system, which watches that verification and checks it before lining the "piece" to finish the exchange. Gatherings included are guaranteed that members have screened and affirmed the exchange.

The procedure not just eliminates misrepresentation, for example, twofold spending or spams, additionally exchanges subsidizes basically, securely, and quick.

# BLOCKCHAIN

## 17 Blockchain Applications That Are Transforming Society

**Blockchain Business**

**Budgetary Services**

Customary frameworks have a tendency to be unwieldy, mistake inclined and maddeningly moderate. Go-betweens are frequently expected to intercede the procedure and resolve clashes. Normally, this costs stress, time, and cash. Conversely, clients discover the blockchain less expensive, more straightforward, and more compelling. Little ponder that a developing number of money related administrations are utilizing this framework to present advancements, for example, shrewd securities and keen contracts. The previous consequently pays bondholders their coupons once certain prearranged terms are met. The last are computerized gets that self-execute and self-keep up, again when terms are met.

Cases of blockchain monetary administrations

- Asset Management: Trade Processing and Settlement

Conventional exchange forms inside resource administration (where parties exchange and oversee resources) can be costly and unsafe, especially with regards to cross-fringe exchanges. Each gathering simultaneously, for example, agent, overseer, or the settlement administrator, keeps their own records which make noteworthy wasteful aspects and space for blunder. The blockchain record lessens mistake by encoding the records. In the meantime, the record streamlines the procedure, while wiping out the requirement for middle people.

- Insurance: Claims preparing

Cases preparing can be a baffling and difficult methodology. Protection processors need to swim through fake cases, divided information sources, or relinquished arrangements for clients to express a couple of – and prepare these structures physically. Space for blunder is tremendous. The blockchain gives an ideal framework to chance free administration and straightforwardness. Its encryption properties enable safety net providers to catch the responsibility for to be safeguarded.

- Payments: Cross-Border Payments

The worldwide installments area is mistake inclined, exorbitant, and open to illegal tax avoidance. It takes days if not longer for cash to cross the world. The blockchain is now furnishing arrangements with settlement organizations, for example, Abra, Align Commerce and Bitspark that offer end-to-end blockchain fueled settlement administrations. In 2004, Santander ended up noticeably one of the primary banks to combine blockchain to an installments application, empowering clients to make global installments 24 hours per day, while clearing the following day.

**Shrewd Property**

An unmistakable or immaterial property, for example, autos, houses, or cookers, from one viewpoint, or licenses, property titles, or organization shares, on the other, can have shrewd innovation implanted in them. Such enrollment can be put away on the record alongside authoritative subtle elements of other people who are permitted proprietorship in this property. Savvy keys could be utilized to encourage access to the allowed party. The record stores and permits the trading of these keen keys once the agreement is confirmed.

# BLOCKCHAIN

The decentralized record additionally turns into a framework for recording and overseeing property rights and in addition empowering the shrewd contracts to be copied if records or the savvy key is lost.

Making property keen declines your dangers of running into extortion, intercession expenses, and flawed business circumstances. In the meantime, it expands trust and proficiency.

Cases of Blockchain Smart Property.

- Unconventional cash loan specialists/hard cash loaning

Brilliant contracts can reform the conventional loaning framework. For example, eccentric cash banks (e.g. hard cash banks) benefit borrowers who have poor credit with required advances – while charging two to 10% of the advance sum and asserting their property as security. Excessively numerous borrowers fall into liquidation and lose homes. The blockchain can undermine this by enabling an outsider to credit you cash and taking your savvy property as security. No compelling reason to demonstrate the loan specialist credit or work history. No compelling reason to physically handle the various reports. The property's encoded on the blockchain for all to see.

- Your auto/cell phone

Primitive types of brilliant property exist. Your auto scratch, for example, might be furnished with an immobilizer, where the auto must be initiated once you tap the correct convention on the key. Your cell phone too will just capacity once you write in the correct PIN code. Both work on cryptography to ensure your proprietorship.

The issue with primitive types of shrewd property is that the key is typically held in a physical compartment, for example, the auto key or SIM card, and can't be effectively exchanged or duplicated. The blockchain record tackles this issue by enabling blockchain diggers to supplant and imitate a lost convention.

- Blockchain Internet-of-Things (IoT)

Any material question is a "thing." It turns into a web of things (IoT) when it has an on/off switch that interfaces it to the web and to each other. By being associated with a PC arrange, the protest, for example, an auto, turn out to be something beyond a question. It is presently human individuals, human things, and things-things. The expert firm Gartner says that by 2020 there will be more than 26 billion associated gadgets. Others raise that number to more than 100!

How does the IoT influence you? Your printer can naturally arrange cartridges from Amazon when it runs low. Your wake up timer will change your time for blending espresso, while your stove will create an impeccably planned turkey for Thanksgiving. These are quite recently a few illustrations. On a bigger scale, urban communities and governments can utilize IoT to create cleaner situations, more proficient vitality utilize thus called 'shrewd urban areas,' to enhance how we live and function.

**Where the blockchain comes in**

As in all cases, the blockchain record gives security to this Internet of things. With billions of gadgets connected together, cybersecurity specialists stress how to ensure this circulated data remains secure.

# BLOCKCHAIN

What can organizations do to shield their frameworks from being attacked?

- How would inventors be able to shield their thoughts?
- How should governments shield their mystery data from spies and potential fear based oppressors?

At that point, there's the issue of how to arrange and examine this huge measure of information that is originating from these related gadgets.

Enter the blockchain record framework that guarantees that data is just acknowledged and discharged to confided in parties. The record awards parties an administration stage for breaking down the immense measures of information.

## Cases of Blockchain Internet-of-Things (IoT)

- Smart Appliances

A brilliant machine is a gadget that associates with the web and gives you more data and control than some time recently. For example, a code associated with your machine can be connected to the web and caution you when your treats are prepared or if your clothing has ceased. These cautions keep your apparatuses in great condition, they spare you cash in regards to vitality productivity and enable you to control your gadgets when far from home, among different advantages. Encoding these apparatuses on the blockchain ensures your possession and empowers transferability.

- Supply Chain Sensors

Sensors give organizations end-to-end perceivability of their production network by giving information on the area and state of the provisions as they are transported the world over. Starting at 2016, a Deloitte and MHI report reviewed 99 driving store network organizations and found that sensors were utilized by 44% of these respondents. Eighty-seven percent of these enterprises said they plan to utilize the innovation by 2020. The innovation is required to develop to 1 trillion by 2022 and to 10 trillion sensors by 2030, as per this sme Deloitte and MHI report. The blockchain stores, oversees, secures and exchanges this savvy data.

**Keen Contracts**

Keen contracts are advanced which are inserted with an if-this-then-that (IFTTT) code, which gives them self-execution. All things considered, a middle person guarantees that all gatherings complete on terms. The blockchain postpones the requirement for outsiders, as well as guarantees that all record members know the agreement points of interest and that authoritative terms actualize naturally once conditions are met.

You can utilize brilliant contracts for all kind of circumstances, for example, budgetary subordinates, protection premiums, property law, and group financing understandings, among others.

**Cases of Blockchain Smart Contracts**

- Blockchain Healthcare

Individual wellbeing records could be encoded and put away on the blockchain with a private key which would give get to just to particular people. A similar procedure could be utilized to guarantee that exploration is led by means of HIPAA laws (in a safe and private way). Receipts of surgeries could be put away on a blockchain and consequently sent to protection suppliers as confirmation of-conveyance. The record, as well, could be utilized for general medicinal services administration, for example, directing medications, control consistence, testing comes about, and overseeing human services supplies.

- Blockchain music

Enter issues in the music business incorporate possession rights, sovereignty circulation, and straightforwardness. The computerized music industry concentrates on adapting creations, while proprietorship rights are regularly ignored. The blockchain and shrewd contracts innovation can circuit this issue by making a thorough and exact decentralized database of music rights. In the meantime, the record and give straightforward transmission of craftsman eminences and ongoing disseminations to all required with the names. Players would be paid with advanced cash as indicated by the predefined terms of the agreement.

- Blockchain Government

In the 2016 decision, Democrats and Republicans scrutinized the security of the voting framework. The Green Party required a describe in Wisconsin, Pennsylvania, and Michigan. PC researchers say programmers can fix the electronic framework to control votes. The record would keep this since votes progress toward becoming encoded. Private people can affirm that their votes were numbered and affirm who they voted in favor of. The framework spares cash, incidentally, for the administration, as well.

The blockchain record, likewise, gives a stage to what we call "responsive, open information." According to a 2013 report from McKinsey and Company, open information – unreservedly available government-sourced information that is accessible over the web to all natives – can make the world wealthier by $2.6 trillion. New businesses can utilize this information to reveal false plans, ranchers can utilize it to perform accuracy cultivate editing, and guardians can examine the reactions of solution for their debilitated youngsters. At the present time, this information is discharged just once every year and is, to a great extent, non-receptive to subjects enter. The blockchain, as an open record, can open this information to nationals at whatever point and wherever they need.

**Cases of Blockchain Government**

- Public esteem/group

The blockchain can encourage self-association by giving a self-administration stage to organizations, NGOs, establishments, government offices, scholastics, and individual residents.ABatherings can associate and trade data on a worldwide and straightforward scale – consider Google Cloud, yet bigger and less hazardous.

- Vested duty

Savvy contracts can guarantee that electorates can be chosen by the general population for the general population with the goal that legislature is what it's intended to be. The agreements indicate the electorate's desires and voters will get paid just once they do what the electorate requested as opposed to what funders fancied.

# BLOCKCHAIN

- Blockchain Identity

Regardless, online organizations thoroughly understand us. A few organizations whom we buy from offer our personality subtle elements to promoters who send you their advertisements. The blockchain hinders this by making an ensured information point where you scramble just the data that you need applicable individuals to know at specific circumstances. For instance, in case you're setting off to a bar, the barkeep just needs the data that discloses to him you're more than 21.

The blockchain ensures your personality by encoding it and securing it from spammers and promoting plans.

**Cases of Blockchain Identity:**

- Passports

The primary advanced travel permit propelled on Github in 2014 and could enable proprietors to distinguish themselves on the web and off. How can it function? You take a photo of yourself, stamp it with an open and private key, both of which are encoded to demonstrate it is true blue. The identification is put away on the record, given a Bitcoin address with an open IP, and affirmed by Blockchain clients.

- Birth, wedding, and demise testaments

Barely any things are more essential than reports demonstrating you're conceived, hitched, kicked the bucket which open your rights to a wide range of benefits, (for example, voting, working, citizenship), yet blunder is overflowing. Up to 33% of youngsters less than five years old have not been issued a birth testament, the

UNICEF revealed in 2013. The blockchain could make record-keeping more solid by scrambling birth and passing accreditation and engaging residents to get to this significant data.

- Personal Identification

We convey a scope of distinguishing pieces of proof: Our driver's permit, PC watchword, personality cards, keys, government managed savings ID, et cetera. Blockchain ID is a computerized type of ID that is built to supplant every one of these types of physical recognizable proof. Later on, fintech researchers say you'll have the capacity to utilize the one advanced ID for joining at any enlistment center. It is open source, secured by the blockchain, and ensured by a record of straightforward record.

**Summary**

It's essential to take note of that for the blockchain to work, the hub to-hub arrange must be roused and consent to work under moral principles. Once, and just if, these principles are clung to, the blockchain could turn into a capable device for enhancing business, leading reasonable exchange, democratizing the worldwide economy, and supporting more open and reasonable social orders.

# Chapter 9: Blockchain innovation myths

**7 Myths About Blockchain**

Blockchain is on the ascent, however there is a ton of deception out there

There are numerous myths circling about the Bitcoin Blockchain, the greater part of them proliferated by individuals that accept excessively and make quick judgments without truly knowing...

Entirely ordinary you may think for a rising troublesome innovation to incite such extraordinary responses and conclusions. Clearly some don't need Blockc

hain to succeed and that others are as yet terrified of it, looking just to shield themselves. And after that there are the sharks hoping to profit from Blockchain by imagining they have the appropriate responses, despite the fact that 6 months back they couldn't spell Blockchain.

So here are a portion of the regular myths you will hear and perused about Blockchain...

**ONE: Blockchain is Immutable – WRONG.**

The Blockchain (record) itself is not unchanging. It is a myth. Unchanging nature in truth originates from the consumption of exertion (for this situation power and figuring assets) identifying with the Proof of Work calculation where the trouble increments and number of Bitcoin rewards for Miners diminishes at regular intervals. As of now 12.5. A definitive noticeable Proof of Work illustration is the Pyramids in Egypt, which took decades to finish and those that went up against the venture needed to nourish and water countless individuals that thusly moved mountains. Along these lines showing Proof of Work fulfillment including extraordinary trouble and use of assets.

Diggers exhaust not just enormous exertion and assets, they likewise put noteworthy measures of capital in Mining hardware to mine the standard cryptographic forms of money. This is altogether different to the Proof of Stake speculation/vested approach. Excavators make the interest in figuring and electrical energy to settle the undeniably difficult (troublesome) PoW calculation (SHA256) to attempt to get a match, called Hashing. This is utilized to check exchanges and empower another Block to be composed on (taking 10 minutes) for which they get a reward. It is a race and mining power directly affects the outcome.

**TWO: Smart Contracts are Smart and they are Legal archives – WRONG once more**

Shrewd Contracts are moronic. They are not contracts by any stretch of the imagination. They are scripts as programming code that are sent onto the Blockchain at a specific address (information store) that take after basically guidelines regularly activated occasions, e.g. On the off chance that, THEN proclamations. They are regularly composed as an exchange direction and depend on the Computational Capabilities of the Ethereum Blockchain.

Shrewd Contracts wipe out the requirement for people to deal with tedious and exorbitant business forms. They are self-ruling and once stacked can't be ceased or adjusted. Like an infection they can work alone

(self-sufficiently) or in conjunction with other Smart Contracts, Data Stores as Oracles and interoperate with other heritage frameworks.

Keen Contracts are not contracts in any legitimate sense, nor will lawful contracts be a piece of Smart Contracts. Be that as it may, they are fit for executing terms (as guidelines) that may live in an understanding between parties, to make an installment or move privilege/possession and exchange stores. They shape some portion of the business rationale layer that connections pleasantly with the procedure rationale to frame what wind up noticeably unintelligent gatherings of exchanges.

Brilliant Contracts are rising and the improvement and arrangement is extremely mind boggling. They are defenseless against assaults/hacks and they are the place the greater part of the current issues, for example, the DAO have been. Savvy Contracts convey exchange directions and progress toward becoming layers and gatherings of Smart Contracts that cooperate to shape another era of Decentralized applications or Dapps.

Keen Contracts alongside Keys (Public and Private computerized fingerprints) assume an expanding vital part in the plan of Blockchain Operating Models where center business forms are robotized utilizing installed Smart Contracts. They are inevitably implanted as firmware into physical things in an IoT world, with everything kept in touch with a record of Everything. Savvy Contracts is the business rationale layer that coordinates the exchange activity between the members.

A Smart Contract does not frame any lawful status, and the legitimate position is to a great extent insignificant. Should a Smart Contract accomplish something the gatherings had not planned. Make a wrong installment? Who is capable? Is it accurate to say that it was hacked or quite recently poor coding?

**THREE: Bitcoin system can be closed down – WRONG**

Investors and perfectionists by and large don't care for Bitcoin for the essential reason of Openness, Transparency, and on the grounds that it is for the most part Free (small scale expenses), contending secrecy permits miss-utilize. Bitcoin is not claimed by anybody. The Bitcoin Foundation gives oversight however not control. Bitcoin is presently 7 years of age and a week ago got through the $640USD resistance. It is now develop.

The code is Open Source and anybody can download it and set himself or herself up as a Miner to mine Bitcoin. Others may download Bitcoin as customers onto their advanced mobile phones as Bitcoin Wallets to execute Peer 2 Peer with whomever they need, passing Bitcoin tokens over the system and not by means of any focal control or body, similar to a clearing bank or focal specialist. Frictionless and where the exchange is ensured and quick.

Bitcoin is for the general population, keep running by the general population, and, similar to the Internet, ca

nnot be closed down - in spite of the fact that there are, obviously, endeavors to police it, with others that need to control it. It is past the focal specialists (Regulators, Clearing Banks and a few Governments) that see the Libertarian danger of Bitcoin and dread it. It is oversight safe, without geological limits. Numerous legislatures are beginning to see the potential and need to be a piece of its development, as sovereign governments race to be first to issue obligation on the Blockchain, and send their own digital currency. To be one of the principal matters.

The other myth is that once the 21 million of Bitcoins are mined the cash will fall and stop and individuals will lose their esteem. The last coins will be mined in 2140 and given there are 9 decimal spots to play with the Bitcoin digital money will do fine and dandy.

**FOUR: There are 20 or 30 Crypto-monetary forms available for use – WRONG once more**

Indeed there are more than 800 digital currencies and inside a couple of years there will be 5,000 to 10,000. There are numerous Crypto Exchanges far and wide, and the number is expanding all the time with more than 20m Bitcoin Wallets now taking care of multi advanced and fiat monetary forms.

The main digital forms of money remain Bitcoin, which has a market top moving toward $12billion, Ethereum with Mkt Cap $1billion, Ripple, Litecoin, Ethereum Classic, Monero, Dash, Augur, MaidSafeCoin, Nem, Waves, Steem, Dogecoin, Factom, DigixDAO, Lisk, Gulden, Synero, Stojcoin and numerous, some more. www.coinmarketcap.com is an incredible place to discover them.

Given the reason for an 'advanced tokenized rail', they depend on numerous times of cryptography considering, late Innovations, and the Computer Science leap forward that made the Distributed Ledger Technology or DLT, that for me takes the brakes of trade. They are a basic piece of the center outline and their utilization relies on upon the business result looked for.

Each Crypto money is utilized for an alternate reason, framing the premise of the security show. The crypto keys are a piece of the exchange to be approved by the Miners, and where every exchange once Hashed is hung on duplicates of conveyed records hung on the system hubs, where Miners hold a full duplicate of the Ledger giving Blockchain its Zero Downtime qualities.

Some are outlined as trade tradable advanced monetary forms, others as tokens, some to compensate and to convey usefulness as a feature of the forked code that endeavors to convey a particular level of execution. Zero Cash or Zcash endeavor (begins mining now) to offer what Bitcoin has with greater obscurity. Others are a piece of a forked plan to enhance the scaling or bolster an alternate accord calculation.

Numerous digital forms of money will never achieve the volumes required to wind up standard. ETHER or ETH was truly composed as a major aspect of the Ethereum arrangement to remunerate Miners and Coders for their computational endeavors known as Gas. Subsequently the expression Gasing Up your Smart Contracts, as wasteful and ineffectively composed code not exclusively is computationally more costly, they are additionally open and vulnerable.

**FIVE: That Bitcoin and Ethereum are the same – WRONG**

Bitcoin was planned as a Peer 2 Peer budgetary framework utilizing the center code in light of the Satoshi papers of 2008. It was planned as a borderless budgetary (installment) framework outside the ability to control and control of national banks, governments and retail banks that take unbalanced expenses for doing practically nothing. Bitcoin was the first and is the biggest Public Blockchain.

Ethereum forked the first open source code and ran live in 2015 with its own particular beginning square, when Vitalik Buterin built it to convey an entire advancement condition around a worldwide Computational Machine, that may one day turn into the new Internet. Ether arrived Jan 2016 and things truly took off.

Ethereum offered surprisingly a Turing complete dialect (an improvement situation) to work out engineering for Smart Contracts that can keep running as a Blockchain Operating Model. Ethereum conveys the fate of trade and where the cryptographic money as a budgetary rail is an outcome and not the core interest.

They share basic elements; they began from a similar source code, they are both a system (P2P), a money and an innovation.

**SIX: The Bitcoin Blockchain has been hacked – again in fact WRONG**

The basic Bitcoin organize has not been hacked. The Bitcoin Exchanges have been hacked - Mt Gox rings a bell - and some were controlled by a few people whose thought processes might not have been open.

Brilliant Contracts have been hacked to change their rationale yields, in the primary to redirect assets to an alternate address, the DOA for instance. In any case, Cold Stores holding key data have additionally been hacked enabling access to programmers that access your Bitcoin Wallet/Account and evacuate the coins.

Individuals who possess and exchange Bitcoin and ETHER have an extensive variety of records, Wallets, and Keys to spread the hazard programmers will record the key logs on Public and Private Keys.

With each fork things are enhancing as pre-generation Use Cases rise.

**SEVEN: Blockchains can't be connected together - WRONG**

Aside from a large group of action to patent parts of Blockchain plan to a great extent by banks, a significant part of the Blockchain people group stays Open Source and focused on enhancing the fundamental execution of the Blockchain code with the goal that it might scale.

Numerous Blockchain new businesses are doing astonishing things to enhance the execution and ease of use of the first code. Consensys, Eris Industries (now Monax), and Tendermint are accomplishing incredible things.

The enormous movement is to interface Chains created, and worked in various dialects and structures (agreement, voting, ways to deal with Identity and so on) and empower the death of Tokens (monetary forms/esteem) between each Blockchain stays complex. Two driving cases of this exertion are Interledger and Cosmos Hub (Tendermint) two such undertakings that are connecting anchors together to make Blockchain eco frameworks and groups, extremely helpful when sent as an Industry Solution.

**Summary**

These are the misconceptions. It is inescapable with any new innovation that there is expansive disarray, and much more so with Blockchain, which is exceptionally mind boggling and includes extremely shrewd individuals planning, creating, and assembling another future where the tenets of exchange are distinctive and where hierarchical working models work in an unexpected way.

# BLOCKCHAIN

The current Forking action is a characteristic advancement prepare, however again those that aren't fans blame Blockchain calling it high hazard, assert it can be hacked, and say Bitcoin is a turbulent cash regardless of it beating everything.

Blockchain is an arrangement of building hinders, an improvement situation to be innovative, to re-outline trade, and to create better approaches for taking care of business issues. Notwithstanding, for me, the most convincing thing about Blockchain is that it conveys the chance to manufacture new Operating Models worked for upper hand as far as cost and proficiency.

Each industry, new creation, anything that individuals don't completely comprehend, are encompassed by Myths, as non actualities as realities, of non certainties and conclusive data. In any case, none of this matters to Blockchain in light of the fact that the general population that know, know and we the Blockchain people group are satisfied about that..!

# Conclusion

The most essential strides organizations can take today is to remain educated on the status and improvement of this innovation. This incorporates the way toward ensuring IT work force are mindful of the innovation, as well as start to end up noticeably familiar with the innovation and genuinely comprehend it. This incorporates understanding what blockchain innovation can reasonably do and what is not plausible. Similarly as with any new innovation, it can frequently be hard to separate between authentic abilities versus la-la-land claims.

Once more, instruction is the way to remaining educated about practical abilities. Another critical stride for the individuals who can profit by blockchain arrangements is to campaign chose and government authorities for adjusted and fitting enactment and directions as examined in the past part. The initial step for governments is to recognize what enactment is important so as to allow organizations and people to take full favorable position of the innovation. The other undertaking for government is to adjust directions that will add certainty to the innovation versus those that will make boundaries to passage and at last decrease advancement. An appropriate adjust is achievable, as well as crucially fundamental for the eventual fate of this innovation.

For scholastics, designers and specialists, the weight is on us to keep on educating the general population, including business pioneers, on the guarantee of blockchain innovation. This requires a genuine appraisal of those things that blockchain innovation does well and real to life revelation while existing, traditional arrangements are more fitting. We should likewise perceive that blockchain innovation is an interdisciplinary examination—

embroiling money, microeconomics, amusement hypothesis, and legitimate hypothesis to give some examples. These are notwithstanding the more evident fields of arithmetic, cryptography, electrical building, and software engineering. At last, the most convincing case for the eventual fate of blockchain innovation is that huge numbers of the brightest and most entrepreneurial people in each of these fields have joined on one innovation—blockchain.

## References

1. Guilio Pristo, "Blythe Masters and Wall Street Opt for 'Permissioned' Non-Bitcoin Blockchains,"

Bitcoin Magazine, Sept 2, 2015,
https://bitcoinmagazine.com/articles/blythe-masters-wall-street-optpermissioned-non-bitcoin-blockchains-1441227797.

2. John Weru Maina, "Lending on the Blockchain with LoanCoin," Cryptocoins News,

https://www.cryptocoinsnews.com/lending-blockchain-loancoin/.

3. List of blockchain startups,

https://angel.co/blockchains.

4. Jose Pagliery, "Record $1 Billion Invested in Bitcoin Firms So Far," CNN Money, Nov. 3, 2015,

http://money.cnn.com/2015/11/02/technology/bitcoin-1-billion-invested/.

5. Daniel Palmer, "7 Emerging Trends For Bitcoin and the Blockchain," CoinDesk, Jan. 14, 2016,

http://www.coindesk.com/emerging-trends-blockchain-bitcoin/.

6. Ian Allison, "R3 Connects 11 Banks to Distributed Ledger Using Ethereum and Microsoft Azure,"

International Business Times, Jan. 20, 2016,

http://www.ibtimes.co.uk/r3-connects-11-banks-distributed-ledger-using-ethereum-microsoft-azure-1539044.

7. Oscar Williams-Grut, "Nine Massive Banks Just Teamed Up to Take the Technology Behind Bitcoin

Mainstream," Business Insider, Sept. 15, 2015, http://www.businessinsider.in/Nine-massive-banks-justteamed-up-to-take-the-technology-behind-bitcoin-mainstream/articleshow/48977655.cms.

8. "Financial Institutions: Blockchain Activity Analysis," Lets Talk Payments, Sept. 7, 2015,

http://letstalkpayments.com/financial-institutions-blockchain-activity-analysis/.

9. "Blockchain Use Cases: Comprehensive Analysis & Startups Involved," Lets Talk Payments,

July 29, 2015,

http://letstalkpayments.com/blockchain-use-cases-comprehensive-analysis-startupsinvoved/.

10. "Know More About Blockchain: Overview, Technology, Application Areas and Use Cases,"

Lets Talk Payments,

http://letstalkpayments.com/an-overview-of-blockchain-technology/.

11. Jad Mubaslat, "5 Bitcoin and Blockchain Startups to Watch in 2016," CoinDesk, Dec. 30, 2015,

http://www.coindesk.com/5-bitcoin-blockchain-startups-watch-2016/.

12. Ian Allison, "R3 Connects 11 Banks to Distributed Ledger using Ethereum and Microsoft Azure,"

International Business Times, Jan. 20, 2016, *http://www.ibtimes.co.uk/r3-connects-11-banks-distributed-ledger-using-ethereum-microsoft-azure-1539044.*

13 "Global Securities Industry Group Survey Finds 55% of Firms Engaging in Blockchain Tech R&D,"

Blockchain Finance, March 2, 2016,

*http://blockchain-finance.com/2016/03/02/global-securitiesindustry-group-survey-finds-55-of-firms-engaging-in-blockchain-tech-rd/.*

14 Adrian Lee and KiHoon Hong, "How Blockchain Tech Is About to Transform Sharemarket Trading,"

CoinDesk, Feb. 7, 2016,

*http://www.coindesk.com/how-blockchain-technology-is-about-to-transformsharemarket-trading/.*

15 Anna Irrera, "BAML Prepping Blockchain-powered Trade Finance Test," Financial News, March 2016,

*http://www.efinancialnews.com/story/2016-03-01/bank-of-america-works-on-blockchain-tradefinance-tests.*

16. Grace Caffyn, "What is the Bitcoin Block Size Debate and Why Does it Matter?" CoinDesk, Aug. 21, 2015,
*http://www.coindesk.com/what-is-the-bitcoin-block-size-debate-and-why-does-it-matter/*

www.ingramcontent.com/pod-product-compliance
Lightning Source LLC
Chambersburg PA
CBHW070315230526
45470CB00002B/889